THE PORTAGE POETRY SERIES

SERIES TITLES

Flu Season
Katie Kalisz

Users with Access: New and Selected Poems
Brandon Krieg

Dining on Salt: Four Seasons of Septets
Wayne Lee

Torrential
Jayne Marek

No Trouble Staying Awake
Teresa Scollon

Another Native Tongue
Susan Riley Clarke

Catch & Release
Lauren Crawford

Steelhead
Lauren K. Carlson

The Coronation of the Ghost
Benjamin Gantcher

The Stone Tries to Understand the Hands
Susannah Sheffer

Red Camaro
Dwaine Rieves

Where Babies Come From
Ori Fienberg

Cuttings
Hannah Dow Kombiyil

Forgive the Animal
Sarah Pape

Love as Invasive Species
Ellen Kombiyil

They Were Horrible Cooks
Allison Whittenberg

The New Life
Wendy Wisner

Restoring Prairie
Margaret Rozga

Table with Burning Candle
Julia Paul

A Bright Wound
Sarah A. Etlinger

The Velvet Book
Rae Gouirand

Listening to Mars
Sally Ashton

Glitter City
Bonnie Jill Emanuel

The Trouble with Being a Childless Only Child
Michelle Meyer

Happy Everything
Caitlin Cowan

Dear Lo
Brady Bove

Sadness of the Apex Predator
Dion O'Reilly

New Wilderness
Jenifer DeBellis

Fulgurite
Catherine Kyle

The Body Is Burden and Delight
Sharon White

Bone Country
Linda Nemec Foster

Not Just the Fire
R.B. Simon

Monarch
Heather Bourbeau

The Walk to Cefalù
Lynne Viti

The Found Object Imagines a Life: New and Selected Poems
Mary Catherine Harper

Naming the Ghost
Emily Hockaday

Mourning
Dokubo Melford Goodhead

Messengers of the Gods: New and Selected Poems
Kathryn Gahl

After the 8-Ball
Colleen Alles

Careful Cartography
Devon Bohm

Broken On the Wheel
Barbara Costas-Biggs

Sparks and Disperses
Cathleen Cohen

Holding My Selves Together: New and Selected Poems
Margaret Rozga

Lost and Found Departments
Heather Dubrow

Marginal Notes
Alfonso Brezmes

The Almost-Children
Cassondra Windwalker

Meditations of a Beast
Kristine Ong Muslim

Katie Kalisz's *Flu Season* chronicles her rural family's domesticity with a tender precision that withstands headwinds of memory, love, dread, mourning, and the quotidian. The opener, "Tending the House," foreshadows the whole, its extended metaphor figuring the entire book, which is "ripping the ivy from the brick walls." In various forms—lyric, narrative, list, ekphrastic, broken-and-scatter-lined, even abecedarian—these poems confront death and illness while celebrating survival and joy through subjects as contrary as giving haircuts and weathering the pandemic, squishing caterpillars and reliving poverty, fileting a fish and treasuring a radish. Hidden in that ivy: "birds' nests, wasps' nests, once, even a snake."

—D. R. JAMES
author of *Mobius Trip* and *Flip Requiem*

To love is to accept the inevitability of loss, as Katie Kalisz reminds us. Even in the warmth of home, the security we long for eludes us: the threat of danger is ever-present, like a gun nestled in a bedroom drawer. But joy is here too, deepened by its impermanence. Flowers tilt their faces to the sun, a couple swims beneath an Indian summer sky, and, in the midst of a pandemic lockdown, children put on a circus. Overflowing with equal parts of love and dread, Katie Kalisz's new collection is a book that speaks to the courage required to live in an uncertain world.

—EMILY TUSZYNSKA
author of *Surfacing*

Using a perfect balance of craft and metaphor, Katie Kalisz weaves her superb poetry collection into a seamless tapestry that embraces our deepest fears, joys, and longings. *Flu Season* tackles the hard experiences of loss--whether it be the death toll of COVID-19, a neighbor's terminal brain cancer, or water contamination from PFAS—but also embraces the deep love of life and family that act as powerful talismans against the darkness. In "The Woodcutter I Live With," Kalisz deftly moves from a methodical observation of her husband cutting wood to a closure that is filled with transformation: "A little smoke. / A little danger. Bringing / him a glass of water / feels like inventing fire." These epiphanies abound in Kalisz' work. She doesn't need artifice to impress as she gives us "the symmetry / of the bones, even the space between / the bones..." And with that honesty, her poems speak a clear language in pure song.

—LINDA NEMEC FOSTER
author of *Bone Country*

Katie Kalisz's finely wrought book of poems, *Flu Season,* is a book haunted by illness and the malaise of contemporary life. Its five sections take the reader through various crises that define the book's parameters: flu, COVID-19, isolation, mortality, fear of loss. If that sounds like a daunting read, fear not: Kalisz finds solace and joy in the midst of these difficulties. There is humor here, and good spirits, and some transformative moments of domestic life that offer, in Robert Frost's words a "momentary stay against confusion."

—PATRICIA CLARK
author of *O Lucky Day*

Life is dread plus maintenance. Dread drapes itself over us perennially. Maintenance is ubiquitous. It's hard to be human. Katie Kalisz, in her uncannily subtle, unassumingly courageous collection *Flu Season*, affirms that even during our good days wherever we walk, work, play, or just stare out the window we're enwrapped in worry. Kalisz's gentle, deceptively masterful writing creates an accessible experience that startles us into realization after realization that one must ignore dread's distraction of "what could happen" to maintain family, spirit, home, the checkbook, the backyard, joy. Early on we realize Katie (May I call her Katie?) is not longing for a better life; she does not want our sympathy when the days overwhelm; she neither rejects nor accepts this life of day after day. She lives within it because she loves within it. In lines perfectly pitched and musically phrased, Katie Kalisz humbly comforts us as she enables us to realize that maintenance with ever-present dread is love.

—JACK RIDL
author of *Saint Peter and the Goldfinch*

Flu Season

poems

Katie Kalisz

CORNERSTONE PRESS
UNIVERSITY OF WISCONSIN-STEVENS POINT

Cornerstone Press, Stevens Point, Wisconsin 54481
Copyright © 2025 Katie Kalisz
www.uwsp.edu/cornerstone

Printed in the United States of America by
Point Print and Design Studio, Stevens Point, Wisconsin

Library of Congress Control Number: 2025932477
ISBN: 978-1-960329-88-2

Cornerstone Press titles are produced in courses and internships offered by the
Department of English at the University of Wisconsin–Stevens Point.

for my mom and dad

ALSO BY KATIE KALISZ:

Quiet Woman

CONTENTS

PART THREE · RED CIRCLES

PART FOUR · STRONG MEDICINE

"The changes we dread most may contain our salvation."

—*Barbara Kingsolver*

PART ONE · GETTING WARM

Tending the House

We replace the deck boards rotting
in the corners, pull away periwinkle
strangling the other flowers in its
eagerness for sun, clean out leaves
that crowd the gutters, sweep sand
collecting on the floor, wipe window
sills thick with dirt, and dust off cobwebs
clinging to the screens carried up from
the basement. Sprinklers sputter to life,
gasping for water. All the twigs and branches
blown down in the storm need raking off the
roof. Ripping the ivy from the brick walls
is akin to stripping wallpaper, but it reveals
birds' nests, wasps' nests, once—a snake.

The Painted Flags

Segue to this sagging rag
it flies over a city   agog   with self-
published art and self-help admiration   This city protests
at protests
for decent causes   and so presents pages   and pages
of shaggy canon   Some of us here   we gag
on reality of sameness   the sag in our flag   the self-
centered brag and
blah and

bluster   Some of us rummage
and slide by   just blend in
by wearing beige   playing tag under eggy moonlight
Those some are not a sum
to change the flag or   bag the sagging
saggers   We wait

for grains of salt and sand
we set up shop near
seedy herders   Wait for wool and when
and whistle   We wait for a whistle to blow

The Woodcutter I Live With

Doesn't let summer
keep him away from
his axe; the way it breaks
ash into pieces
is a necessary violence
to keep us warm in
winter. He wears long
pants, heavy boots,
gloves, even in the sudden
May heat—pauses
to yell something
to the children, always
aware of where they
play. The spray of
sawdust looks like
confetti, the only sign
of change. His arms
and back accelerate
into a surface that
constantly resists.
The axe moves
in a circle down
his left, over gray
hair. He reaches tall,
springing into his toes,
and forward, all his
weight committing
to each stroke again
and again, the same
futile action repeated,
moments of insanity,
like biting and biting
into a rock. He swings
into something he
almost can't swing

through. It is not like
baseball, connecting
in the sweet spot; there
is no squishy bounce,
no long ball flying
to applause, no easy
follow through here, and
contact happens every
time. A perfect slugging
percent. What does he think
when the axe hits the
wood? Is it anger or
longing? I know he'll keep
swinging until pieces
finally splinter off
and a final swing
splits the log, clean
like a nut. He has an
addiction to heartwood;
he finally rests his heaving
chest, stacks the pieces
in a neat pile. Allium bloom
near the large oak he has
dismantled. A hummingbird
watches him. When he comes
in he smells of sweat and
gasoline. A little smoke.
A little danger. Bringing
him a glass of water
feels like inventing fire.

What My Students Bring to Introduce Themselves on the Second Day of Class

Three wrenches, one quite large.
Several coffee mugs.
Pictures, keys, books,
rusty scissors.
A liter of apple juice, empty.
A bottle of honey,
also empty.
Headphones, colored pencils,
a probation officer's card.
A metal lunch box, a round rock,
a wooden
spoon.
A whoopee cushion. Yes,
really.
A tiny Speedo, flicked
onto the desk in front
of him. Extracted wisdom
teeth in a small yellow
envelope that stays
sealed
for now.

Anniversary Poem

Cream in the pitcher.
A scoop of sugar in your mug.
The red tea kettle on the burner.
Two blue chairs.

Sit here with me. Draw your chair
nearer. Reach toward
your right side.
My left hand reaches too.

The scratchy surface of your face.
Silver shoots of hair, heat.
Our tangled bedsheets witness
two happy sighs.

Hear the quiet river water.
Black tree shadow.
A soft, light midnight.
My pink skin seared with bliss.

Wrap yourself around me.
Be my hide, while I burrow
further into
your warm life.

October Windstorm

Thin shouldered, the house shudders
while darkness outside cloaks the bricks
in a lace shawl. Things snap:
tree branches, the water clicking the large rock,
a tongue of wet leaves licking the gutter.

At the window, tree silhouettes stretch and twist
around shadows of themselves, freed
from a bondage of calm and released into chaos.
Closer to the house, a dusky rabbit squats beneath
the birdfeeder, filling herself on spilled seed,

windblown ears pinned close to her head,
pressed fur waving welcome, warning.

Missing Sleep

Mornings we trade off our baby girl,
you rising at four to dress your tired body in the dark,
meet other fathers for a run that makes you more
awake, an illusion of a longer life, a more productive day.
Alone in bed, I listen to her grunt and kick out of
the blanket you swaddled her in hours earlier,
sounds indignant and growing
louder, stronger, more.

I let her struggle while I fight off the risk:
deeper sleep that beckons I forget
what lies in the white bassinet by my feet,
until I finally rise after you've been gone
not half the hour. I uncoil her from the light
cotton blanket, her volume mounting
like a gathering cavalry, her stretch
a question for the dawn about the day.

She coughs and coos, missing sleep
or food, while I think of you on your run, trying
to know the ache of your knee, the burn of your calf,
your breath on the crisp May air.
Propped up on our dark bed, I listen
to the sucking sounds while the sky aches
through the windows and around the trees,
a red ember, stealing into our home.

Home Haircuts

Finally,
we take the clippers
from grandma
down
out of the cupboard,
put the teal cape
over the shoulders,
set up
outside
on the deck.
And suddenly,
these boys
I know
so well
seem like strangers
below me.

I am unprepared
for the intimacy
of their neck
hairs,
standing on end.
The back of the ear.
Skin reacting
pink and hot. At the hum
of the machine,
my hand
trembles.
I see the start
of tan lines
around their t-shirts,
a frontier of white skin
where the sun
hasn't reached.

I remember
the last time
I did this, trying
to save money,
before the children
arrived,
twelve years ago. Then,
we were
on the deck too,
but it was fall,
and the October winds
swept the hair away
before it hit the boards.
The next spring,
we found it
in the charcoal grill,
woven into a nest
that the mice had made.

When I take off
the cape, and look
at these small
men, through their masks
of freckles,
I'm not sure
who
they have become.

The Day my Father Followed John Kerry into the Men's Bathroom at Chicago O'Hare

He never flew, my father, but when
my brother hedged at driving cross-country
just the two of them, he found a reserve
of must somewhere in an old fish bag, bought
a ticket that involved three legs—six take-offs
and touchdowns—and drove himself the four hours
to Detroit Metro's mess of an airport to board,
nervous and sweaty, the first plane.

In Chicago, he amused himself by sitting
neatly in his seat, holding onto his one
green bag, listened to Bob Seger's
Silver Bullet Band on his discman,
checking his ticket in hand and the gate
over his shoulder to be sure he sat in
only the right place.

When John Kerry walked across the airport hall
my father forgot his green bag, his memorized
fear. Probably, it looked like he was chasing
while he followed at a quick pace the man
who once ran for President of the United States
into the automated bathroom.

Who knows what they found to talk about—
the cold, the Catholic church, the calamity
of Abu Ghraib?
As my father flew
the two remaining legs—Phoenix, then
Portland—I like to think
he fell asleep, a soft smile of a coup
creeping into his crows-footed eyes,
the lightness of a grey sky as bright
as snow in winter.

To My Valentine, While We Sit Separately at Swim Practice

At least it's warm here—
balmy, and so each time I blink
I imagine our revised honeymoon
on a Caribbean island, one of those
over-the-water bungalows with
a clear floor, in order to see
the colorful fish that swim beneath.
Champagne and pineapple.
Instead, I open my eyes to see
the red and pink jellyfish
on our daughter's swimsuit, as she
butterflies through the chlorinated water;
the electric blue bolts
on our son's lean legs, and his
small muscles clinging to the bones
of his arms as they pull the water down.
We made these creatures! I think
to you—on the carpeted steps
of the viewing area—with all the other
parents around us hunched over
mobile phones, and all the small brothers
and sisters on all their tablets, and
the one woman who knits, and the sounds
echoing off the pool deck. *Little bodies—*
look at these little bodies that we made.
You turn to me—as our children
flip turn into the next 25 yards—
and smile, as if to say, *I love them,*
and *I love you.*

Getting Warm

Sawn probably the day before, they were
on the side of the road, covered in snow. Pale
orange sawdust blanketed the wet dirt. I watched
two boys dust off the heavy logs, carry them one
at a time to the open trunk of a white
Trans-Am, a large mouth awaiting food.
The small trunk filled with two or three
good pieces, not even enough warmth to boil
a kettle on a home fire. Home,
my woodpile is stacked with five cord, a roof
over the logs to keep them dry and eager
when they get a chance in the flame. I have
been there, on the side of a shoulderless
road, parked on iced over gravel and wearing
a thin hand-me-down jacket, hauling wood
with bare red hands that chap and crack
but keep on hauling. I hated the cars passing
us, watching us, as though only poor people
get cold. A rose garden of hate just bloomed
inside me. That's how I became warm.

Warnings

Weather, of course: flash flood, severe
thunderstorm, tornado. The siren goes.
But also riptides, drought, ozone action day,
marine, wind, heat. *More ticks than ever
before!*, shouts the CDC. In my neighborhood—
No Trespassing; Private Property; Silence your
Dog; Drive 17mph or less.
What I tell my children: hands
out of your mouth, don't lick
money, don't pick up that cigarette
butt. They do it anyway, joking. The Surgeon
General tells women not to drink alcoholic
beverages during pregnancy because—the risk,
birth defects. I read it on my beer bottle.
Pillows from Target contain chemicals
known in the state of California to cause
cancer. CNN and NPR advise that what I'm about
to hear, or see, or read is graphic, contains
disturbing images, may trouble some viewers.
Always, my parents: watch out for poison ivy; don't
hit a deer but if you do, accelerate; the gun
is in the top drawer at the cabin; there's a bee's nest
under the fifth stair down to the water.

PART TWO · DREAD

Mom Was Afraid to Plan Dad's Retirement Party Because When She Planned Her Own Father's Retirement Party it Became a Wake

It's why she saves hotel soaps and
shampoos, small glass jam jars from

fancy restaurants she thinks she'll never
return to. Why she had to look

under my bed for the invitations to
their surprise 25th anniversary party.

What   she   already   knew,
given to me finally. Admitted.

A sync of my mother's past with
her cautious joy taught me how

to imitate. I collect the same, more: soaps
and shampoos from hotels, Kleenex boxes;

names of ghost and future children;
baby teeth my children lose; names of

friends' babies who have died: Anna,
Barbara, Olivia, Grace, Clementine. Black

dresses to wear to my husband's funeral,
some future day; shoes to go with the dresses;

smooth shells from the NC shore, in case
I don't get back before it sinks; walnuts,

wild ramps, more than I can use,
Morel mushrooms that shrivel on the

sill; syndromes: Resignation, Imposter,
Anticipatory Mourning. Once I took an empty

bread bowl from my half-eaten lunch,
wrapped the soggy basin in a napkin,

and stuffed it in my backpack to carry
back to my office to eat in private, later.

I have inherited her planning for loss.
Worry balloons around me, floats like

it's at a party it doesn't know
was cancelled.

Dread

I can feel it rise like a welt
of poison ivy, a crescent shape,
on my thigh. It bubbles, becomes
3D. I uncover it like a fossil
in the children's garden, with toy
broom and plastic shovel.
I camp out in a gray fold
of my brain, rationing
my supplies, a weak
flashlight that throws
shadows on the wet
and sloping wall. Soon,
regret crawls out like
the frond of an orchid
stays craggy, prehistoric,
or makes its way to a blazing
purple bloom. After all, dread
is inherited, but also
cultivated. Like an orchid,
it needs tending to
in order to thrive.

Osteobiography

Female, aged forty, middle-
class based on calcium and bone
density; coxal bone and eye sockets
reveal shyness, timidity.
Gardener's patellas, likely well-
oiled, but still cracking
each time they squat.

Phalanges show pre-arthritis, nimble
fingers that might have peeled away
nails, candle wax, dried pancake batter
on counters or breakfast tables.
Left ring metacarpal is smaller, shows
signs of long marriage.

Jaw bone has a propensity
not for grinding, but clenching –
holding onto things, which corroborates
the knuckles' wear.

The adult teeth appear older than
they are. So serious.

Two dozen elastic ribs
and unusual grooves
in the radius and ulna—perhaps
remnants of carrying something
like firewood. Sternum still warm
and pink.

Cranium: ringed like the inside
of a tree, lined by thoughts that
etched themselves into circular
patterns. A worrier. Clear
as salt water.

Smooth metatarsals of a walker, not a runner.
Hips that orbited out with children,
three, perhaps four, perhaps more.

No breaks anywhere, not even remains of
a hairline fracture, so pretty
cautious, possibly even
paranoid.

Searching for How to Fill the Time

Each day since May's entrance I have
wiped the deep freeze clean of cat hair and
hot afternoon dew from an open door.
Stocked with hard meats, extra supplies
in case of visitors who are usually
planned for. The bed is tucked up
by 8.04 like a jar of frozen strawberries,
waiting to be used, wanting
for warm toast, sweet cream.

Mail truck at 12.16 marks the morning leg
for this miser accounting minutes of the sun
lifting on one side of the house passing
overhead, sinking to signal the nearing end
of a solitary day so deliberate, it self-destructs
in my oval palm. I release it toward
the neighbor's large unshaded yard, expanding

over protected trees and fish. My stockpiled time,
like the bourbon my husband sips cautiously,
is an uprising that abides by tally-taking truth:
we count the cords of wood we have yet
to store instead of the cords we have stacked.
The mash and the barrel in his one
glass lasts him the six-hour evening.
I pour an ounce for myself, always afraid
we'll run out.

Shade

Under a rippling canopy of lithe branches
your knobby knees like poles
holding up the trees, the sky
you lie on your back, hands behind head
knees bent
the way you used to thinking hard
about something fun.

No landscaping to escape from,
no patio furniture,
no margarita filled pitcher with six
                    matching glasses
                    —and before
the divorces, miscarriages and twins, cancer,
solemn remission.
Before we learned how to hide our sunburn
lines, hide how white our skin was.

Is it enough? The dead
and matted grass of early spring
giving way to summer leaves, warm
soft earth that dries out
breathes in, cleans up,
sometimes.
Enough means running
   but not from being chased.

Is it enough?

Calling Unemployment Once-A-Week in Michigan

If you make a mistake you may start over
Bead of sweat   seconds tick   wind
blows

Were you physically able and available for work each day?
Nod. Press small "1" on keypad.   You are not excused;
you will be asked an additional question.

Did you make an active search for work as directed
during the week you are now claiming?
You are not excused.   Nod. press small "1" on keypad.

Did you refuse any offer of work or fail
to go for a scheduled job interview?   (interview interview interview)

Mirage of rippling water in August humidity.

You will be required to provide   (even if you have not actually been paid).
Shake.   Press "2" on keypad.

Did you or will you receive   (you will be required to provide)
holiday pay from your regular employer for any day of the week?
If you are not sure
shake
and press "2."

Did you or will you receive   (you will be required to provide)
vacation pay of the week you are claiming? Press "2" on keypad.

Did you or will you receive pay   (you will be required to provide)
in lieu of notice or termination pay for any day
of the week you are claiming?
If you are not sure   you are not excused.

Did you work in self-employment?

Did you work for any employer last week?   (you will be required to provide
Shake.

> Not even one?
> Not even part time?
>> *Did you perform duty*
>> *in the Military Reserve*
>> *or National Guard*
>> *for more than 72*
>> *consecutive hours?*

Shake.

> Did you do anything
>> productive
>>> at
>>> all
>> since
> you last called?

If you are not sure
shake.

Do you expect   (anything) (anymore)   *to be working*
for the same employer next week?   *If*
> *you answer no,*
>> *was your separation from employment due to:*

> *1. Lack of work?*
> *2. Reduced hours due to a lack of work?*
> *3. Being fired?*
> *4. Quitting?*
> *5. Some other reason?*

a. Incompetence
b. Bad luck
c. Poor hygiene
d. Stress at home
e. Such awe at having a job you forgot to work

Did you have any other reportable earnings?
    You will be required to provide   (you will be
        required to provide
            even if you have not actually been paid).
babysitting, lawn-mowing, found pennies, can-collecting

> *If you make a mistake you may start over*
> *If you make a mistake you may start over*
> *If you make a mistake you may start over*

In Flu Season

We fry fish. We wallow and indulge, thrive
and then survive, cling to a toilet, a tissue, a mug
of drugs. The sun is something we were permitted
in our youth, a kind of dessert, but now we starve –
become recluse tending our own fires, isolating
our neighbors in their icy huts. We try to remember
holiday mantras – gifts we gave that made winter
seem quaint: *bread for the year behind, light for
the year ahead or love like the river or there's
no such thing as bad weather only bad clothes.*

The CDC says flu season is October through
May, eight months, spanning football season,
all major holidays except the July fourth,
archetypes of both death and rebirth.

In the small reprieve from flu season,
the neighbor next door succumbs to
brain cancer. An older neighbor hums by
in his red corvette, top down. Another
neighbor in a silver Lexus, hard top
convertible, a twenty-year dream. She
wears her fashion hat while the motor
rumbles beneath her pedicured foot.
A former neighbor has fled after
an affair, a divorce. The adulterous
wife still sits on her porch, smoking,
letting the lawn and flowers go.

I pick ripe tomatoes of early August –
placing imperfect fruits on the counter
saving them from the dog's harvest.
All over the lawn, I rescue his
already-plucked green tomatoes –
prop them on window sills,

summon the sun to
turn them red.
In the fruit bowl,
overripe ones crack and
mold, juice leaking onto
bananas, apples,
contagious.

The November Plot

Indian summer warmth lies
to an already hardening soil.

Only one way to prepare:
still the garden. Brown

from the ground up
yet there are pangs of green, painful

to watch. And painfully they
succumb to the creeping

contagion: cold coming for the roots.
To shorten the suffering, to minimize

the mess of wet and shriveling
shoots where fat slugs foul clean soil,

shears clip away, shortening the distance
from earth to stalk, amputating the

green-tipped waving stems. The last leaves
fall all rust, all brusque. We prepare

for sameness by cutting back
the fastest growing who still

collect the sun, store the water,
efficient as chipmunks.

Only one way to prepare: steel
the body.

Spring does not always arrive
in time.

First Book

I want to bury the boxes
of books in the yard, somewhere
the dog can't dig them up. I want to
do it while it's raining so the pages
get soaked, the ink bleeds out
of the words, the pages return
to their purity. But it is winter. The ground
is frozen. I have missed my chance.
Instead, this book becomes
another child to nurse through
the cold season, through the risk
of flu and other epidemics, under the constant
gray sky. Something else I must
tend and nourish. Something else to lug
around town with me on errands,
in case someone wants to buy a copy, wants to
torture me with attention like I am selling
watches from a gray trench coat.

Bunker

Today, the children dug a ten-foot-deep hole,
a space big enough that they can all fit
inside. They shovel the dirt into their wagon,
haul it away to make a bike jump, using
everything they dismantle. Are they already
better at saving their lives than I am? I have
molded my life to keep them alive, waking
in the night to nurse them through stomach flu
and pneumonia, ear aches, itching allergic
reactions, fevered dreams. Why didn't I think
to hide them underground, where bulbs survive
the winter, where snakes and moles and worms
shelter in place? Why didn't I think to build them
a bunker beneath this troubled world we nurture?

PART THREE · RED CIRCLES

What Rises

The sun, ever earlier
and earlier, a bluebird's
orange belly to the feeder,
a robin beak with a worm,
spikes of iris,
a heron from the mist
off the river.
Flags on mailboxes
up and down the street,
steam from our pot of oatmeal,
the May wood pile with ash
and cottonwood.
Welt of poison ivy
on my ankle, Muscari
in the lawn, and dandelions,
rhubarb stalks, purple heads of asparagus.
A second chicken coop
the neighbors erect and paint blue.
Theodore, the chipmunk, to the
deck railing, for orange peels
and apple cores, the dog's rear end
in a yoga pose, my rear end
in a yoga pose, my son
into a Norway spruce,
the river to meet the bank,
masks to overtake faces,
the death toll.
And at last,
the white moon,
surrendering.

Red Circles

They arrive in red lipstick, hoop earrings,
one wearing yellow pants on his head,

his father's large shoes. He is the clown,
striped and dotted, introducing his older

brother and sister as they instruct him to do.
Somersaults. Pyramids. Amateur magic tricks.

This sounds like a metaphor but it is
not; my children are planning a circus

for this circus season, in the land of circuses
and chaos, circles like citrus fruits,

ever overlapping on the *New York Times*
digital map of the outbreak. The map

that is beautiful if you don't know
what it means. It could be beautiful.

Neighborhood Newsletter, July 2018

I pluck a Petoskey stone from cold water.
The neighbor finds a tumor in his brain.

Poison ivy blankets the hill, hissing.
Constant news on cable television.

Smoke balloons from the outdoor wood boiler.
The neighbor's tumor grows and grows and grows.

The Gypsy Moths

Happily my brother and sister and I practiced our aim
with bicycle tires, an ambush on the driveway where the
gypsy moths caravanned from one side of the yard to the other,

searching the oak and aspen of our childhood sylvan for
a transient home. We tried to get our tires at
a right angle to their lined bodies, pedaled quickly

to make a neat cross or an addition sign and,
mastering that, we lined our tires up to roll over
their length like the lowercase "L"s we practiced

on the dot-lined penmanship paper during school.
How the green and yellow streaks of their guts
trailed out behind their furry spotted bodies.

Sometimes, they would become circular splats
that we tried to forget, even though we sped around
the circle driveway to see again the remnants of life,

paintings made with bodies that we couldn't imagine
once alive. Maybe if they'd been moths earlier.
Caterpillars begot butterflies. Something crawling became

something beautiful that flew. Our childlike version of the
resurrection's confounding annual mystery, even then we knew
the fatigue of staying in one place long enough, a recurring accumulation

of death and flight and infestation and no difference made.

Bee Sting

Just as I pulled my hand back from
the smooth skin of a beech tree, I was
stung by a bee for the first time in my

life. I didn't know what it was—the sting
of the sting. It's been forty years, I'd started

to wonder if maybe I *had* been stung before,
and hadn't known it. Maybe I was sting-blind,
I thought. Maybe there was something I could

not feel. My walking companion pulled the stinger
out, a kind of second sting, and a relative stranger so
close to my neck, another sting for a private person.

I waited for my tongue to swell, to feel
if my body would react at all—would rear up
or roll over. The sun speckled the meadow

like a frog's back. A hawk circled overhead,
waiting too. The stinger long gone, I can still sense
the space on my neck where she landed,

plot of my body now a badge from my hike,
a little numb bump. A primitive tattoo marking the
day and time and year and place. Looking forward,

the wind rippled tree leaves and meadow grass.
We walked on, spotting a chipmunk, a deer,
creek water tumbling over a small rock.

June

It used to be when school lets out, when the pools would open,
when Little League starts up and fireflies arrive. Once, June

felt like a redemption love story in a country song. We were all
June brides, myself, my mom, my mother-in-law. Now, June

is also migration season, I hear on NPR, when water is warmer
for refugees to cross oceans in small, flimsy boats. So

while a bride bathes in scented oils, scrubbing her skin
raw, a family straps possessions to a board and wades in the water

to shove off. The bride dries, lotions her body, powders her nose
and chin. The family wilts in the breeze, sends goodbyes to the shore.

The bride is dressed by a modern-day valet, adorned with jewels,
sets a martini on the bible while she fixes her own hair. She prepares

for dinner and dancing and sex in something fancy. All this while
they clutch and sink, swallow seawater instead of wine spritzers.

June is now the human migration season, and we watch from our papers
and radios like animals who are safe enough on the hierarchy, bickering

about the latest way to wear our denim, insisting on double sinks
in the master bath, and honeymooning where they escape from.

Amusement Park

Chaos of screams, bodies jolted
by a downhill toss, across a stretch
of brown grass, bewildered children
searching for lost guardians, oil frying
the dough and potatoes into coaxing
smells, storm clouds framing
the skeletons of seething metal machines.
What amuses us are ornamental lights
adorning the Ferris wheel, manmade hills
of wood that the coaster rolls along,
pink or blue candy that dissolves
as it meets our tongues. Following
a familiar face means surrender when a daughter
disappears in the crowd, when turning a circle
in search turns up a thrill, then a return
to searching until only the sidewalk path
is left, and there we are, closer to the newest
coaster, and the screaming riders captivate
us, like movie sound effects of other people's
horrific absorbing stories.

Midwest Invasions, an Abecedarian

Autumn Olive, Asian Carp,
Butterbur, Barberry, Baby's Breath, lasagna-like
      Curly pondweed,
Dalmation toadflax, exhausting
      Emerald Ash Borer,
Fishhook waterflea, gallivanting
      Garlic Mustard (rather pretty en masse), Gypsy Moth,
Honeysuckle, Himalayan Balsam,
      invasive idiocies.
Japanese weatherfish, coiling
      Kudzu,
Lyme-grass,
Mile-a-minute weed, and
Norway Maple (the narcissist),
obdurate
      Parrot Feather, & privet, purple loosestrife
quintillions of
      Russian Boar,
Sea Lamprey, Scotch Pine,
Tree-of-heaven,
unnecessarily vigorous
      Valerian,
Wrinkled Dune Snail,
xenografted
      Yellow Floating Heart, and clusters of
Zebra Mussels.

Cleaning out David's Fridge

After we put him on the 6 a.m. train going west,
three of us caravan to his house to clean out
his fridge. It is December. We know he won't be

coming back, and that he couldn't eat much these
last months, but it surprises us, all the food
he's accepted from people trying to do something

for his terminal cancer. It is more than we imagined.
We take turns—reaching in, pouring out, holding
open the garbage bag. We each take what we

think we'll use, still good ham, sticks of butter,
unopened bags of Halloween candy,
eleven eggs, sacks of potatoes and onions.

There is so much homemade soup, Tupperware
containers of casserole servings. On my way home,
the milk I've taken spills in the back of the car,

seeping onto the carpeted trunk. I soak it up
with paper towels, scrub it with Oxiclean
and soda water, but the stain is still there, like

on an old recipe, a memory of the morning David left
while we chased after the train, waving to our reflections
in the black window, our footprints marring the fresh snow.

Candy Cigarettes

One
I learned to smoke from
candy cigarettes, how to play

baseball from Big League Chew
and Fun Dip. I practiced getting

married with Ring Pops and bartending
with Vernors. I grew up next door to

the Manistee National Forest and
down the road from a gas station

that kept a black bear in a cage for
customers. So you could stay longer,

they served Blue Moon ice cream from
a walk-up window. It was called

Thirsty's and it's still open, selling
gas and liquor. Lotto tickets.

Two
Lately, my children get twenty dollars
and sugar cookies every few months for

donating their blood to science because
a company dumped waterproofing chemicals

nearby; they test and retest our well,
our blood, for the toxic plume of PFAS.

Each month we receive eight plastic barrels
of water, light blue and gurgling.

I thought I chose an idyllic
home for my sweet children,

on a small river, with a large
yard and plenty of wild animals,

native plants, owls and herons
nesting nearby, and snapping turtles.

Three
Now, the language is all
that's beautiful. The hand gestures

the EPA workers use on
the local news are a dance;

legalese is multisyllabic and filled
with liquid consonants, high-frequency

vowel sounds. Like decay, it dresses up
in sugar and sparkles.

Four
Samantha, the bear, died and they
finally removed her chain-link cage.

Later, the state cut bear hunting licenses.
Since then, the black bear population

has grown by 88%, which sounds good.
There are signs for seven miles on that

stretch of road that borders the national
forest, warning drivers of bear crossings,

but semis still collide with one every now
and then. It doesn't even make a headline.

What Falls

The swollen river, back
into its banked boundaries,
stalks of tulips and daffodils,
the heavy globes of peony heads,
burdened pregnant with bloom.

Hair from a pony tail, beads
of sweat, helicopters from
the maple tree, drip coffee,
dependably. All the petals
on the flowering trees of spring
like showering a new bride.

Rain from thunderstorms, weakened
tree branches in the strong gusts
of wind. Birdseed from the feeder,
empty bottles and empty ice cream tubs
into the recycling bin, and mail through
the slot. The belly in breath. The bank
account. The number of strokes.

Children, from bikes and skateboards
skinning elbows and knees. Laundry
from the line. Demand for energy.
Carbon emissions. Glass from shattered
windows. Stars for the wishers. Finally,
the rate of new cases, and so
the time we have only together.

PART FOUR · STRONG MEDICINE

Strong Medicine

On the way back from
        Grand Marais, after too many
dirt roads, once
the rain had started up
again, more
        heavily,
the October colors
intensified like a stronger dosed
medicine for muscle
ache, an elixir
for incessant
        cough.

Color invaded
        my veins. Inflamed
by passage to this place–
        thick cut rare land between
mild summer and wild
    fall, dizzying,
                infected. I was
    a fever brewing, and then broken.

Wet Wood Smoking

after the painting Wood Fire *by Andrea Kowch*

The day is damp, with lingering snow banks
and the silk scarf tied around her neck is
silly. Her unmarried hand carries a collection
of kindling, as though the fire has already gone
out and the task is to bring it back somehow
before darkness arrives first. Her other hand
is at her side, or in her pocket, staying warm.
The buttons at the neck of the green coat are
undone, the hair undefined from the clouds,
and behind her, a barn, but not red, unlike her nose,
her cheek bones. Four crows gather around the
snowbank, perhaps waiting for a mouse, perhaps
already having one. A fifth flies over. In the damp
a train whistle presses its muted call against
every blade of golden prairie grass, flattening
the field. The house is behind us, and she has
to walk through us to get to her fire. She looks
through us, as though we are already snuffed out,
like the fire, already washed away in the smoke
or the fog.

Terminal

While the neighbor dies, I wear my swimsuit.
The kids shriek from the river, hoist a crayfish
onto a boulder to study, examine a tiny spider
spinning a web from his behind.
While the neighbor dies, the sun shines,
the sprinklers go on, the tomatoes ripen.
I eat lemon cake, with ivory rosettes and orange
marzipan. I pour a glass of wine. While the neighbor
dies, the sprinklers go off, the hummingbird
sucks at the canna lilies, paddlers kayak down the river,
past his house, his bedroom window, where he is dying.
While the neighbor dies, mosquitoes live, the mailman
delivers the mail to the living who are folding laundry,
shopping online, emailing, and posting on Instagram.
While the neighbor dies I buy sweet corn
at the farmer's market, the kids color, his own son
goes waterskiing, the hibiscus blooms.
My children plant their pits from peaches and plums.
I sunbathe, in my swimsuit. While the neighbor dies,
a plane crosses overhead, ferrying him away to
a different terminal.

Twelve Ash Trees

Twelve ash trees fall
the week before Easter. All by the river,
the Monday after baptizing our youngest son,

in the year that a new pope
is chosen, the year we are
twice violently sick. I have seen

the diseased trees—with lines like worms
along the bark, and then how the bark hangs loose,
before falling away from the limbs,

revealing the smooth and pale wood—
old skin under a Band-Aid—frail and white
beneath. Only the bark doesn't grow back,

and the trees become hollowed out.
It's tough to tell how hollow they are.
One just falls—without notice or care.

Like an attack. Our Lenten penance
is enduring the stomach flu.
We have been lax about meatless Fridays,

indulging in breakfast chorizo,
Jimmy Dean Maple, an afternoon
cheeseburger as we criss-cross town

en route to an errand. We are frantic—
three children under four, working
for them and at real jobs, thinking we are

sacrificing ourselves for our babies—giving time
like water, like milk. How we underestimate
the wrath of God. The virus ravages us.

We are all left like the trees,
bore through by a beetle, our bark
not fitting us anymore.

Hospital Poem

My grandfather and his dog are on
the same medications, and I confuse who we are talking
about, whose heart is fluttering, whose leg
is weak, whose skin is drier than it should be,
a side effect. We clutch hands while a machine
beeps, sounding like a toy my son has. At home,
I would take out the batteries. Say they died.
The toy is sure to follow. Here, a new noise comes
from the bed alarm, which I would like: an alert when
one of my children arises, my daughter, the sleep
walker, before she opens the locked door and wakes
everyone: my husband reaching for the shotgun, expecting
an intruder; my son, the prowling cat in a dark house
arriving silently at my bedside, staring. I stare
at the flyaway hair on this old man's head,
the slipper socks that adorn his feet, the slack skin
around his elbows. Leaving the hospital, I kiss his
liver-spotted forehead, the same way
I send my daughter off to school, or into evening.

Filleting a Fried Trout

(ars poetica)

At the base of the tail
slip the last tine of your fork beneath
the speckled skin, crispy now and then
slit it toward the head, to peel back the skin.
See the white meat in small neat trapezoids.
Take the fork; use the tool. Look at the fish
on its plate, perpendicular to your own face.
Gently, gently, press the fork tines into
the fillet's centerline, inviting the meat away
from the bones. Then, the other side. All this
for the reward of the spine.
Lift the delicate tail, like a petal, like lace,
carefully, carefully, just enough so that
each fine fish bone slips singularly away from
the bottom fillet. Now you have a small skeleton,
something that looks to belong in a natural
history museum, not your trash can.
Hold it up. See the beauty in the symmetry
of the bones, even in the spaces between
the bones, in the way it all holds together
after being caught and cooked and picked clean.

Candlesticks

for Matt's wedding

This was the nicest gift we received for our wedding.
I am handing them to you now, without the adornments
of wrapping paper, gift bag, bow. I am handing them to you now,
the silver warmed from my own hands, the metal close to my skin
these last hours I sat holding them on my lap near my belly, on the way
to you, like the warming of the necklace my young daughter gives
back to me after she keeps it circling her neck during
displays of dress-up, pretending. These candlesticks have
the spilled wax of our first years together, dinners that I burned,
or he did, sometimes despite great and long trying, sometimes
on purpose, for a lesson not learned. They are not
polished; there is no time for that. But I have protected them
by putting them up, away from the new puppy's teeth in a dark closet
where they seemed to shine in small light when the door was opened
to retrieve the vacuum cleaner, the grocery coupons. It is not
that we want to be rid of them. They are still dear to us:
how they surprise the meager macaroni on our already yellow plates!
If you bring them out for meals, you will find each other more
forgiving. If you polish them together, rubbing away our spent trials
and errors, you may start your marriage from a farther-in place, beyond
the general traps of most sightseers who visit the usual ruins.

Drive-through Coffee Shack

We pull up next
at the small window where
a blond woman, hair in a pony,
silver earrings gleaming,
wears an oversized sweatshirt.
The inside of the house seems so
desirable. I wish I could
crawl toward the glowing
center, crawl through the open
car window, crawl into her arms,
live there for good.
It is mysterious and yet
I know exactly what I'll find.
I've made it up. I'm sure I'm right.
It is not
the car, not this outside world,
not something too big and unknowable
and watery.
Little coffee house, on Highway 101
at the edge of the ocean,
take me in, show me home, be my constant
steady supply of
dark, rich, hearty, warm, thick, muddy, lasting,
wake-me-up, kick-start my day, last through supper
and all this rain,
love.

Syrup-Making

I distill the rhyme
            of tap
and sap, mapping maples
on the forty-acre plot
    snowshoes plodding me
                    above the powder and
blue tubes like jumbo veins   running
        from one tree heart
    to another.
            We boil pots
                    of the sweet   clear
        fluid on our wood stove
downstairs
            until,
                        skimming the bottom,
        a sugar paste

all that is
        left.

Fernweh*

German for a longing for distant places

My shadow has become cavalier,
farsick for places she has never
visited: Aruba, Anguilla, Venus.
She leaves me earlier each day
to lie down in the shade, little
puffs of white dandelion fluff
poking through her torso and
eye sockets. An ant crawls
the line of her lips where a
smile should be. A bird pecks
at her open palms.

PART FIVE · HUSH NOW

A Temporary Stay

after the painting Sojourn *by Andrea Kowch*

It's not the wild hair, or the white farm turkey,
or the butterfly nets filled with wind, or even

the ruffles on the pretty dresses. It's not the black
swallowtail butterflies landing on the big heads

of Queen Anne's lace, not the lace collars
that the sisters wear. It's the open window

on the second story of the house behind them where
I pause. The curtain billows out of it, like the nets,

blowing the same direction. The yellow fields match
the yellow hair, aglow, already lifting off into the sky.

It's a scene between seasons, on the cusp of change,
waiting. The last of something. Like us, it's impermanent

– the girls will go back inside later, the wind will die down,
the day will draw to its end, the window will close.

The butterflies will alight to a different field. We will all
leave soon enough. Let us sojourn here a little while longer.

Love in the Time of COVID-19

Is a new record player
on Sunday morning,
Eric Clapton's
S l o w h a n d playing
while I have coffee
and a star-shaped
cinnamon biscuit.
Rain on the porch's
metal roof, and pelting
the river's surface.
Pale pink tulips
that have survived
the late freeze.
Green grass and a
gray sky and the dog
whimpering for a walk.
A new BB gun to
take out the cowbirds.
Cards from the kids
calling me their safe place
with phonetic spelling and
little dots of syrup.
Seeing my mom from
a distance, through
the car window—
her strawberry hair
and soft skin.
Trading her my
old magazines
for soup in jars
and a tin of cookies.
Handing her hot coffee.
Learning she still has
my baby teeth.

How the Woman in a Blue Oldsmobile Quarantines

for Michelle

She's taken to driving out into the country,
letting the new baby sleep to the lull
of the breathy engine. She tries not to stop
fast, to avoid the squeal of the aging breaks,

instead, rolls through stop signs, tempting
hidden hills, and double yellow lines. The fruit trees
blossom ridges into tufts of white and pale pink,
like a girl's nursery. She passes a corner sign

that says
>   *Lunch*
>   *Beer*
>   *Donuts*
in that order, sips a red bull from a straw,

sets it down on old crumbs in the cupholder.
The Potluck Pick-Up trash caddies
dot driveways, while the small dog sleeps
in the sun on the front passenger seat, atop

unopened bills and Valu-mailers for self-storage
and leaf-guard gutters. She knows what she owes,
just has to wait on the unemployment line
to get through, has to conjure up something

for dinner from the back of the cupboard, has to
keep the kids busy with a pine cone craft project or
a candy cane leftover from Christmas. And she will.
She always does.

The New Year

May in the Midwest
means the new year
has finally arrived.
It only begins when
winter ends. We all wake
from dormancy, and parents
tote babies around,
nests appear, like new construction
and everything greens.
All the May flowers
that April delivered
tilt their faces
to the altar of the sun.
We revisit what we hoped
for back when the world
was dark. We have more time
now, more daylight, to drink outside
and read encyclopedias and count
the stars on the tattered flag.
Now is the time for
all we thought we could do
back in January,
for all we thought
we should do, but never
did, dreamed, but could not
wake for.

Let Me Tell You About My Friend, David

He was the nicest guy, talked to anyone,
traveled by train, mostly, because he

liked the sound of the cars rattling
together. Most people grow petty,

but not David. No, he kept us in line—
made us see the good in the people

we gossiped about. Carved us
little wooden boxes and let us hammer open

geodes for Christmas presents, scratch off
Lotto tickets. Loved baseball and maps, shopping

thrift stores, seafood subs. He'd mix
7UP with white zinfandel, and he made

the best cobbler, any kind of fruit. To him,
every lady was pretty. In his living room

he set up a model train track instead of a sofa.
He was kind of a hippie, made a peace sign

out of rocks in his front yard, cultivated
fruit trees, and drove a mint green Prius,

had a skinny gray pony tail, painted.
He was born in January and

died on the last day of the year,
really getting his money's worth.

Used up the time and left. No partial taxes.
That was David. About this pandemic

he would have said something like—well, actually,
I wonder what he would have said.

I can see his face, and hear his voice, but
I can't make out the words.

Almost March

Blankets spill over
from couch to carpet to
kitchen floor. A dog's
lonely footprints smudge
the front sidewalk. River
ice palms small divots
of pooling water—
we even go for a tromp
through the packing snow
smell the hint of dirt, almost
grass, almost March, the mercury
above freezing, everything melting
almost like ice cream—
that sweet.

Prayer Before the After

for my husband

I already weep owl-eyed
how it would be without
you in the already small world
smaller than unseen and gone from
    my perch of self, of life,
my neck twisted only back or
silent aching wingbeats in aimless swoop
around the yard
preying on, prey of
our prized past.

Share the sickness I will get, your memory loss
(pray for contagion, for collusion)
and we'll both hunt a heaven or starve our way
into dusk on a few more Sundays.

Now no knowing when or what
only who,
only who,
when the fine print blurs,
after
and then the surviving begins
only how
only how
without you?

River Swim

Cold is a distant vapor on green currents
my body buoyant and mine alone

while neighbors gaze at our playful ritual,
your gaze a grateful gleam. We swim upriver

to delight in the glide downstream
through a small rapids feet first

navigating rocks and holding hands
around the bend that shows us home.

Sounds of lawncare, children, the nearby
roadway are muted by water growing

in our ears, hair swirling like slow-motion
seaweed. On either bank, a silent movie

of an Indian summer day plays but we watch
the screen of sky reel clouds overhead,

attend separately to happiness,
hope it dries on us slowly, curing.

Still Life

She is concerned as a practiced prayer,
an evergreen crown adorning her
head and wisps of white hair barely
visible beneath a gauzy veil tied
under her chin. Her gentle concern
emanates through furrows of old but firm
skin, liver-spotted, drooping eyelids still open
and searching, poised mouth about to whisper
perhaps, *why?* into his large ear.

He attends her by memory,
steadies worry with a clutch: dirt-stained
hands grasp the searching palm
the soft white skin
of her shrouded knowing and
unknowing, forgetting, repeating,
retelling, unfolding, returning
regretting, forgetting.
In some small need again
patiently he intercedes.

Radish

The pleasure of finding one red radish
in the dense green foliage my father called
a garden was a ticket into his just praise,
my small system of effort, reward,
accomplishment I could finally arrange.
We'd sit at the table in the kitchen, look
for birds he told us were rare, and wait for him
to bite into our plucked radish, halfway through
his sandwich that mom had made, again.
We waited for the way his eyes would close
just after the crunch into it, then the glimpse
of white meat inside the thin red skin, so exotic
to the three of us who still held close our naïve
palates for foods, thoughts, acts. Imagine
the taste we conjured from his face
wrinkled in tan content, to be home for lunch
eating food he had grown, harvested by his children
and given to him like jewels we had formed
in our sandbox.

Hush Now

In my dream, I bake a prayer
with little metal teaspoons
and chanting, eyes closed, to
raw dough until small bits
of bread appear.

I pluck a tree like a ripe carrot,
holding the base of the trunk
with my thumb into the earth,
my hand gripped, ready.

I make a sanguine soup, a balm
for sore hearts and shoulders,
and I comb your hair
with a doll's miniature brush—
tell you everything will be ok.

Once I heard a priest say:
"We are persecuted
with cynicism; we erupt
with selfishness; resist
the temptation
of discouragement."

I used to think
discouragement was
a punishment, not an
indulgence. But now I see
I was wrong. We linger

too long on cable tv—
red and blue banners
flying news that is always
breaking, always broken,
shattered shells I scatter along
the front fence, warning neighbors.

See how the leopard frogs glimmer
in the sun? Hush now—here is a lullaby:
forage in the woods, swing on the tire swing,
rocking to sleep, like we live between the pages
of a hymnal, and any moment now, someone
will open it to find us here, content.

ACKNOWLEDGMENTS

Thanks to editors of the following journals where these poems first appeared, sometimes in earlier versions:

Amethyst Review: "What Rises"

Big Scream: "To My Valentine, At Swim Practice", "The Painted Flags"

Dappled Things: "The Gypsy Moths"

Drafthorse: "Calling Unemployment Once a Week in Michigan"

Eunoia Review: "Terminal", "Cleaning out David's Fridge"

Gyroscope Review: "Bunker"

Loch Raven Review: "Let Me Tell You About My Friend, David"

Midwest Quarterly: "Dread", "Fernweh"

Mom Egg Review: "First Book"

Muddy River Poetry Review: "Home Haircuts"

OneArt: "Radish"

Panoplyzine: "The Woodcutter I Live With"

Trouvaille Review: "Midwest Invasions"

The Indianapolis Review: "Candy Cigarettes"

The Westchester Review: "Filleting a Fried Trout", "A Temporary Stay"

Thimble Literary Magazine: "Red Circles"

Third Coast Magazine: "Osteobiography"

Third Wednesday: "October Windstorm"

Willows Wept Review: "Hush Now", "How the Woman in a Blue Oldsmobile Quarantines"

* * *

Many thanks to the wonderful team at Cornerstone Press; to Pierce Cedar Creek Institute, The Writers' Colony at Dairy Hollow, and the Elizabeth George Foundation for time and space and funding that supported these poems; to writers David Cope, Barbara Saunier, and GF Korreck for being my early readers and for their encouragement and good humor; and to my husband and my children, always.

KATIE KALISZ is a Professor in the English Department at Grand Rapids Community College, where she teaches composition and creative writing. She holds degrees from the University of Michigan, Loyola University of Chicago, and Queens University of Charlotte. *Quiet Woman*, her first book, was a finalist for the 2018 Main Street Rag Poetry Book Award. She is the recipient of a 2023 Elizabeth George Foundation Grant, and her poems have been nominated for the Pushcart Prize and Best of the Net. She lives in Michigan with her husband and their three children.

www.ingramcontent.com/pod-product-compliance
Lightning Source LLC
Chambersburg PA
CBHW030500130626
46549CB00007B/2793